AMISH
Canning & Preserving

AMISH
Canning & Preserving

How to Make Soups, Sauces, Pickles, Relishes, and More

Laura Anne Lapp

Good Books

New York, New York

Good Books books may be purchased in bulk at special discounts for sales promotion, corporate gifts, fund-raising, or educational purposes. Special editions can also be created to specifications. For details, contact the Special Sales Department, Good Books, 307 West 36th Street, 11th Floor, New York, NY 10018 or info@skyhorsepublishing.com.

Good Books is an imprint of Skyhorse Publishing, Inc.®, a Delaware corporation.

Visit our website at www.goodbooks.com.

10 9

Library of Congress Cataloging-in-Publication Data is available on file.

Cover design by Peter Donahue
Cover photo by iStockphoto

Print ISBN: 978-1-68099-456-8
Ebook ISBN: 978-1-68099-459-9

Printed in China

TABLE OF CONTENTS

GETTING STARTED

Growing up Amish, the eldest daughter in a family of seven, canning and preserving were always a part of family life, a part of summertime that went hand in hand with gardening. Now, as a mother of four growing boys with a large garden, I still find canning and preserving a part of my summer tradition. I love gardening, and preserving the beauty of my garden is just another part of that tradition.

Canning and preserving can be hard work, but with the right equipment and some time spent in the kitchen, you will reap the benefits of your labor all winter long. There's such a wonderful feeling of satisfaction placing your gleaming jars on shelves or cupboards and knowing that it was your efforts that put them there, and for me it's knowing exactly what's in those jars. No artificial ingredients at all, just fresh food from my garden. I still buy fruit from local orchards (as we don't have fruit trees), but that's okay, as I still know where the food's coming from.

There are some items you will need before you begin, but most are fairly inexpensive, and you can reuse them year after year. I recommend buying new jars for your first season of canning. That way, you won't have to worry about chips around the outer edges or cracks anywhere in the jars. If the outer edge of a jar is nicked or chipped, the jar won't obtain a tight seal.

Jars are available in quart, pint, or half-pint sizes. You can also buy even smaller jars, what I call jelly jars, which hold approximately ½ cup. I can all my pickles, applesauce, peaches, pears, beets, and tomato juice in quart-sized jars. My jellies, sauces, salsas, and relishes go in pint-sized jars, but we are a family of six and eat lots at every meal. You can use any size jar that works well for your family.

New canning jars (or mason jars, as they are usually called) come complete with lids and rings, also called screw bands. Lids are flat and have a rubber seal on the inside rim that conforms to the top of the glass jar and seals tightly in the canning process, preserving your food. Lids can be bought separately and are typically used only once. Screw bands do not have an infinite lifespan like jars; they get bent and sometimes rust—even now—and they need to be replaced as they wear out.

The recipes in this book are all processed using a boiling-water-bath method. You can also use a pressure canner, but I don't have one myself and have never used one, so I didn't feel comfortable using that method in my book, and water-bath canning has always worked well for me. You will also need a canner or hot-water-bath canner. A canner is basically a large stockpot, so if you have a large pot, you don't necessarily have to buy a canner. I often use my stainless-steel twelve-quart kettle as a canner.

A jar lifter is a handy tool that you will use often while canning to take your jars out of boiling water, so it is a necessity.

A canning funnel is not necessary but recommended, especially when canning sauces or fruits. I like stainless-steel funnels as they don't stain or melt.

A canning rack is also recommended to keep your jars off the bottom of the pot away from direct heat. Most canners come complete with the rack, but if you're using a pot, you can use a cake cooling rack or can tie screw bands together to make your own rack. In a pinch, I sometimes use a clean dishcloth on the bottom of the pot for my canning rack. It keeps the jars from clattering as they boil and also keeps them from breaking.

It's important to heat your jars before you fill them, not to sterilize them (as they will sterilize during the canning process) but to reduce the stress of temperature change. The best way to heat them is in hot water. Some people recommend heating them in your canner, by placing them in water until they reach a simmer (180°F, almost boiling). You can also use your dishwasher, and I've found that washing my jars in hot soapy water and leaving them on the counter to dry is enough to keep them hot, but my kitchen is always extremely warm in the summertime because I have no AC.

If you're nervous about your jars not sealing while in the canner, you can also heat the lids the same way you heat the jars, but placing the lids on warm jars and then putting them in a canner of boiling water has always worked for me. The screw bands never need to be heated, as that's the part that you fasten securely before putting the jars into the canner.

When filling the jars, be sure to follow each recipe's instructions about headspace, or the space between the top of the jar and the top of the food. Sticky foods like canned fruit or applesauce can cause quite a mess if the jars are too full. Most recipes require ½ inch of headspace, although soft jams or fruit juices require a little less.

After the jars are filled with food, be sure to wipe the surface, especially the outer rim, clean of all food residue or particles. Not doing this step correctly can prevent a tight seal from forming during the canning process.

When all the jars are filled and the screw bands are fastened just fingertip tight (do not use a tool or device to tighten them), place your jars in the canner and adjust the water level so that all the jars are covered, and process at a full rolling boil according to the recipe's instructions. When the jars are done, remove them carefully using the jar lifter. Place them on your kitchen counter or sturdy surface, and don't move them for 24 hours. At this time, it's not necessary to dry the jars or remove the screw bands. After 24 hours, you can remove the bands, check for a tight seal, and wipe down the jars.

Any jars that haven't sealed can be kept in the refrigerator and enjoyed within a few days. Food safety concerns related to this would seem to be dependent on what was being canned; one wouldn't want to eat, for instance, chicken soup if it had been sitting at room temperature for at least twenty-four hours.

Store your jars in a cool, dark space such as a pantry, cupboard, or basement. Basement storage is ideal for canned foods as the temperature is often cooler and more consistent.

Home-canned food is generally considered safe to eat for one year. I have kept food for up to two years and it's been fine, although the taste is not quite as good. It is important to label all canned food with dates to facilitate using them in a timely fashion. If you notice any discoloration or mold growing in your jar, obviously that food is not safe to eat anymore. Any food that is opened and not consumed right away *must* be refrigerated. After the vacuum seal is released, the food can spoil quickly just like fresh food.

I hope you enjoy this book and all the fruits of your labor.

A note on yields:

I've found that lots of canning recipes yields are only approximate. It's hard to say exactly how many quarts, pints, etc. you'll get from one recipe, so as you're canning please remember that the yield won't always be just what the recipe says.

A note on the recipes:

The recipes in this book are all recipes that I or members of my extended family have used or still use every summer when preserving the bounty of our gardens. I hope you enjoy them and return to them year after year, just as I do.

Fruits

Preserving Fruit

One of the easiest ways to preserve fresh fruit is using a syrup. The fruit is peeled (usually), then sliced or halved and put into jars. The type of syrup you make depends on your tastes. Sugar helps fruit keep its flavor and texture, so traditionally heavy syrups with lots of sugar are used, but it's really not necessary to use all the sugar. You can even use unsweetened fruit juice or water, but please note that if you do use water to can fruit, the fruit will not keep its shape and color or flavor and may look a little discolored and have a bland taste.

A heavy syrup is made up of equal parts water and sugar, so it's easy to adjust to taste. To make a syrup for fruit, measure water and sugar to your taste into a large pot. Bring to a boil, stirring until sugar is dissolved. Turn heat to low and keep syrup warm until ready to use. The yield will be approximately 1 to 2 cups of syrup per quart of fruit.

Canning Fruit

To can fruit, start with ripe fruit that has no spots or blemishes. Any fresh fruit that's ready to eat raw is ready to can. The procedure for most fruit is the same. Wash fruit well; peel if using peaches or pears, and remove stems if using cherries or berries.

Pack the fruit into clean jars allowing plenty of headspace. My own rule of thumb is never packing past the first "ring" from the top of the jar (that's what I tell my boys when they help me). Pour sugar syrup over fruit, again leaving headspace of at least ½ inch. Canned fruit can boil over, and that makes quite a sticky mess, so follow a basic hot-water-bath canning procedure to process. Most fruit should be canned for 20 minutes.

APPLESAUCE

Applesauce is the main fruit I can, usually three bushels every year. Amish people traditionally serve applesauce at all meals except breakfast. It is served as a side to almost everything, even soup. My own family eats applesauce with their pizza. My husband grew up eating it that way, and now our boys prefer that, too. I just smile and watch them dip their pizza in their applesauce. Ginger Gold or similar "sweet" apples need less sugar than more tart ones such as the Smokehouse variety, although in recent years I've done Smokehouse apples and they make delicious applesauce! You can also use a combination of apples to suit your tastes.

Yield: 1 bushel of apples for approx. 25 quarts

1. Wash apples well and remove stems. If using a Victorio strainer, there's no need to core or peel, but if you want completely "clear" applesauce with no specks, it's better to core and peel the apples.

2. Cover the bottom of a large pot with water about 2 inches deep.

3. Pour prepared apples (cut into fourths) into pot and bring to a boil.

4. Boil until soft and fluffy.

5. Very carefully (apples will be *hot*) press apples through Victorio strainer/food mill. The resulting puree should have a nice smooth consistency.

6. After apples are pureed, add sugar to taste and stir well.

7. Ladle applesauce into jars, leaving plenty of headspace (at least ½ inch or more).

8. Process in hot-water bath for 20 minutes.

BLUEBERRY PIE FILLING

Canned pie filling is a great product to have on hand in the winter. It's so easy to open a jar for desserts or pies.

Yield: approx. 9–10 pints

3 quarts fresh blueberries or other berry of choice (washed and picked over)
I quart + I cup cold water, *divided*
3 cups sugar
1½ cups clear jel (or therm-flo)
Combine berries, I quart water, and sugar.

1. Bring blueberries, water, and sugar to a boil over medium heat.

2. Mix clear jel (or therm-flo) with 1 cup cold water.

3. Stirring constantly, add to berry mixture.

4. Boil until thickened.

5. Ladle into clean jars.

6. Process in hot-water bath for 20 minutes.

CHERRY PIE FILLING

Yield: approx. 9–10 pints

7 cups + 1½ cups cold water, *divided*
5 cups sugar
3 quarts pitted sour cherries
1¾ cups clear jel (or therm-flo)

1. Bring 7 cups water, sugar, and cherries to a boil over medium heat.

2. In a separate bowl combine 1½ cups cold water and therm-flo.

3. Add to cherry mixture, stirring well, until cherries are thickened.

4. Ladle into jars.

5. Process in hot-water bath for 20 minutes.

APPLE PIE FILLING

Yield: approx. 8–9 pints

6 cups + 1 cup cold water, *divided*
4 cups sugar
1 tablespoon cinnamon
1¾ cups clear jel (or therm-flo)
6 quarts fresh apples, peeled and sliced

1. Bring 6 cups water, sugar, and cinnamon to boiling.

2. In a separate bowl combine 1 cup cold water and therm-flo.

3. Slowly add clear jel (therm-flo) mixture to boiling sugar mixture, stirring constantly.

4. Pour mixture over apples, and stir to combine.

5. Ladle into clean jars.

6. Process in hot-water bath for 20 minutes.

FRUIT PUDDING (OR MUSH)

Fruit pudding is a very simple Amish dessert that is great on its own or poured over ice cream. It's simply fruit juice of your choice, thickened with therm-flo. You can also add fresh fruit before serving.

Yield: approx. 9–10 pints

3 quarts fruit juice of your choice (grape or raspberry are especially delicious)
3 quarts water + extra for therm-flo
4 cups sugar
2½ cups therm-flo

1. Bring fruit juice, 3 quarts water, and sugar to a boil.

2. In a separate bowl mix therm-flo with enough water to make a smooth paste.

3. Add therm-flo to juice mixture, stirring constantly.

4. Boil until thickened.

5. Ladle into clean jars.

6. Process in hot-water bath for 15 minutes.

Tomatoes

A note on lemon juice in tomato products:

Food safety organizations recommend adding 1 tablespoon bottled lemon juice per pint of tomato product and 2 tablespoons per quart. I never use lemon juice in my own tomato products and have never had a problem, but if you prefer to do so you can always add it in as an added precaution.

A note on therm-flo:

Therm-flo is a modified food starch that works well in canning recipes as a thickener. It is usually mixed with water to make a paste, then added to tomato products to thicken them. If you don't like the idea of adding starch to your product, tomato paste is another option to thicken home-canned tomato products. Therm-flo is always available at Amish or Mennonite bulk food/grocery stores, and I'm sure it's available online, too.

STEWED TOMATOES

Yield: This recipe can be adapted to any size jar.

tomatoes, enough to fill your jar of choice
1 heaping tablespoon chopped onion
1 heaping tablespoon chopped green peppers
1 heaping tablespoon chopped celery
1 tablespoon sugar
1 teaspoon salt

1. Peel and quarter tomatoes.

2. Fill jars with tomatoes.

3. To each quart add all remaining ingredients.

4. Process in hot-water bath for 1 hour.

HOT SAUCE

Yield: approx. 2–4 pints

1 pound tomatoes
1 pound hot peppers of your choice
1 pound onions
1 teaspoon salt
½ cup white vinegar
1 teaspoon garlic salt

1. Wash and cut up tomatoes, hot peppers, and onions.

2. Mix in all remaining ingredients and bring to a boil over medium heat.

3. Cook until soft.

4. Press through Victorio strainer or tomato press.

5. Ladle into jars.

6. Process in hot-water bath for 30 minutes.

TOMATO SOUP

This recipe makes a condensed soup. To serve, add an equal amount of milk (or to taste). This is an old family recipe that my mother always made. It's mildly flavored and delicious paired with grilled cheese.

Yield: approx. 8–10 quarts

14 quarts tomatoes, sliced (not peeled)
3 quarts + 2 quarts water, *divided*
7 medium onions
14 stalks celery
14 sprigs parsley
2 cups flour
3 cups brown sugar
½ cup salt
1 cup butter, melted

1. Cook tomatoes in 3 quarts water until soft.

2. Cook onions, celery, and parsley with 2 quarts water until soft. Vegetables need to be soft enough to pass through a Victorio strainer or food mill.

3. Strain cooked vegetables and pour juice into large stockpot.

4. Whisk flour, brown sugar, and salt together.

5. Add melted butter and enough cold water to make a nice thick slurry about the consistency of cake batter.

6. Stirring constantly, whisk flour mixture into tomato juice mixture.

7. Bring to a boil and boil for 1 minute.

8. Ladle into jars and process for 1 hour in hot-water bath.

CHILI BASE

Yield: approx. 20 pints

12 quarts tomatoes, peeled
12 onions, chopped
2 bunches celery, chopped
1 cup salt
3 cups vinegar
7 cups sugar
3 peppers or more to taste, chopped
1 tablespoon black pepper or more to taste
1 tablespoon cinnamon or more to taste
1 tablespoon allspice or more to taste
1 tablespoon ginger or more to taste

1. Mix tomatoes, onions, celery, and salt.
2. Let set at room temperature for 8 hours or overnight.
3. Add all remaining ingredients.
4. Bring to a boil.
5. Ladle into jars.
6. Process in hot-water bath for 30 minutes.

Note: This is a sweeter chili base, so feel free to adjust seasonings to your own tastes

(BASIC) TOMATO JUICE

This recipe can easily be adapted to suit your taste or needs. See page 26 for a more seasoned variation of this basic recipe.

Yield: approx. 3 pounds tomatoes for 1 quart juice

1. Heat tomatoes until soft enough to pass through a food mill or Victorio strainer.
2. Bring tomato juice to a boil and add seasonings of your choice.
3. Ladle into jars.
4. Process in boiling-water bath for 15 minutes.

SEASONED TOMATO JUICE

Yield: approx. 4–6 quarts

½ bushel tomatoes
5–6 bell peppers
3 large onions
7 stalks celery (leaves and all)
¼ cup salt

1. Cut up vegetables.

2. Bring to a boil.

3. Cook until soft enough to pass through Victorio strainer or food mill.

4. Bring juice to boiling and add salt.

5. Ladle into jars.

6. Process in hot-water bath for 15 minutes.

HOMEMADE V-8 JUICE

Yield: 6 quarts

6 quarts tomato juice
¾ cup sugar
2 teaspoons onion salt or more to taste
2 teaspoons garlic salt or more to taste
2 teaspoons celery salt or more to taste
1 teaspoon salt or more to taste
½ teaspoon pepper or more to taste

1. Bring all ingredients to a boil.

2. Ladle into jars.

3. Process in hot-water bath for 30 minutes.

PIZZA SAUCE (VARIATION 1)

I make this recipe every summer. I use it for other things as well as pizza, such as spaghetti or lasagna. For more pizza sauce recipes see pages 30 and 31.

***

Yield: approx. 6–7 pints

9 pounds fresh tomatoes (or enough to make 13 cups tomato puree)
½ cup lemon juice, fresh or bottled, *optional*
2 teaspoons dried oregano or more to taste
1 teaspoon ground black pepper or more to taste
1 teaspoon salt or more to taste
1 teaspoon garlic powder (or minced garlic to taste)

1. Wash tomatoes well and remove stems.

2. Add approximately 1 inch of water to a large stockpot.

3. Quarter tomatoes and bring to a boil.

4. Boil for 3 to 5 minutes until tomatoes are slightly soft.

5. Pass softened tomatoes through a Victorio strainer, food mill, or tomato press.

6. Pour tomato sauce into a large stockpot and add seasonings.

7. Boil, stirring occasionally until the sauce is thin

8. Ladle into jars and process in hot-water bath for 30 minutes.

PIZZA SAUCE (VARIATION 2)

Yield: approx. 10 pints

2½ gallons diced tomatoes
8–10 medium onions
4 green peppers
2 cups vegetable oil
½ gallon tomato paste + more to taste
1 cup sugar
2 tablespoons oregano
2 teaspoons pepper
3 tablespoons pizza seasoning
1 tablespoon Italian seasoning
2 tablespoons dried basil
1 teaspoon garlic powder
½ cup salt (or salt to taste)
Therm-flo, *optional*

1. In a large stockpot, bring tomatoes, onions, and peppers to a boil.

2. Boil for 20 minutes.

3. Pass through tomato press or Victorio strainer.

4. Pour puree into large stockpot and add remaining ingredients.

5. Boil for 1 hour.

6. If sauce needs to be thickened, add therm-flo mixed with water or another ½ gallon of tomato paste.

7. Ladle into jars and process in hot-water bath for 30 minutes.

PIZZA SAUCE (VARIATION 3)

Yield: approx. 6–7 pints

6 quarts tomato juice or puree from fresh tomatoes
1 tablespoon garlic
1 tablespoon oregano
1½ teaspoons black pepper
2 tablespoon salt
2 cups sugar
1 package Mrs. Wages Pizza Sauce Tomato Mix
1 cup therm-flo

1. Mix all ingredients, except therm-flo, in a large stockpot.

2. Boil for 30 minutes.

3. Mix therm-flo with enough water to make a paste.

4. Stirring constantly, add therm-flo mixture to tomato mixture.

5. Boil until thickened.

6. Ladle into jars and process for 30 minutes in hot-water bath.

KETCHUP (VARIATION 1)

Homemade ketchup has a completely different flavor than store bought. The consistency is usually thinner and it tastes much sweeter. See page 34 for a different take on this ketchup recipe.

Yield: approx. 8–10 pints

4 quarts tomato juice
2¼ cups sugar
1 teaspoon pepper or more to taste
¾ teaspoon allspice or more to taste
1½ teaspoons onion powder or more to taste
¾ teaspoon cinnamon or more to taste
¾ teaspoon cloves or more to taste
1 tablespoon salt
2 cups vinegar
1½ cups therm-flo

1. Combine all ingredients, except therm-flo, in a large stockpot.

2. Bring to a boil and boil for 15 minutes.

3. Add enough water to therm-flo to make a paste.

4. Stirring constantly, add therm-flo mixture to tomato mixture.

5. Boil until thickened.

6. Ladle into jars and process 30 minutes in hot-water bath.

KETCHUP (VARIATION 2)

Yield: approx. 6–7 pints

4 quarts tomato juice
¾ cup brown sugar
¾ cup white sugar
2 teaspoons dry mustard or more to taste
1 teaspoon ginger or more to taste
1 teaspoon celery seed or more to taste
1 teaspoon pepper or more to taste
1½ teaspoons salt or more to taste
½ teaspoon cayenne pepper or more to taste
¾ cup vinegar
¾ cup therm-flo

1. Mix all ingredients, except therm-flo, in a large stockpot.

2. Bring to a boil and boil for 1 hour.

3. Mix therm-flo with enough water to make a paste.

4. Stirring constantly, add to tomato mixture.

5. Boil until thickened.

6. Ladle into jars and process for 30 minutes in hot-water bath.

SALSA (VARIATION 1)

Yield: approx. 12–15 pints

4–5 quarts tomatoes, peeled, chopped
4 large onions, chopped
1½ cup jalapeños (approx. 6 peppers), chopped
6 bell peppers, chopped
2 cups white vinegar
1½ tablespoons chili powder
½ teaspoon alum
½ cup pickling salt
1 tablespoon garlic powder
1 teaspoon onion powder
4½ teaspoons pepper
⅓ cup sugar
1 (12-oz.) can tomato paste or ½–1 cup therm-flo,
  optional

1. Combine all ingredients, except tomato paste or therm-flo.

2. Bring to a boil in a large stockpot.

3. Simmer for 30 minutes.

4. For a thicker salsa, add tomato paste or therm-flo.

5. Ladle into jars and process for 20 minutes in hot-water bath.

SALSA (VARIATION 2)

Yield: approx. 7–8 pints

14 cups peeled and chopped tomatoes
3 cups chopped onions
½ cup chopped jalapeño peppers or more to taste
2½ cups chopped bell peppers
¼ cup salt
4 teaspoons chili powder
4 teaspoons cumin
1 cup tomato sauce
3 tablespoons brown sugar
6 tablespoons therm-flo
⅔ cup vinegar

1. Combine tomatoes, onions, and peppers.

2. Add seasonings and mix well.

3. Combine tomato sauce, brown sugar, and therm-flo.

4. Stir well and pour over vegetables.

5. Add vinegar and mix thoroughly.

6. Boil for 20 minutes or until thickened.

7. Ladle into jars and process for 20 minutes in hot-water bath.

Pickles

Pickles are one of the easiest and most forgiving things to can. Pickles start with fresh cucumbers that are sliced any way you prefer them: thin, thick, ridged, or straight. If you grow your own, you can pick them when they're tiny and can little gherkin-sized pickles. Most pickle recipes ask for a hot brine to be poured over sliced cucumbers and then processed immediately, so I usually mix the brine and start heating that while I wash and slice the cucumbers. I try to have the brine as hot as possible, not quite boiling, before I pour it into the jars, and also try to have the water in my canner at a full rolling boil before I put the jars into it. Use a jar lifter and be very cautious—I have burned my forearm often!

Many pickle recipes list Mrs. Wages Kosher Dill Pickles mix as an ingredient. This seasoning mix is easily found at many stores that sell canning supplies. I have even found it at Walmart. If you have an Amish or Mennonite bulk-food-style grocery in your area, I'm sure they would have it, too.

Pickles taste best if you wait 2–4 weeks before opening them. I like to refrigerate mine prior to serving, although you don't have to.

Most of the recipes in this section describe different brines, using the same basic instructions for each type of pickle. For most pickle recipes you will need approximately 2 gallons of sliced cucumbers. If you have leftover brine, that's okay. You can always refrigerate it for the next time.

SWEET KOSHER DILL PICKLES

These are my family's personal favorite. I make jar after jar of them as long as my cucumbers keep producing in the garden. We eat them with everything, but especially sandwiches. Grilled ham and cheese on homemade bread with pickles tucked inside tastes amazing!

Yield: approx. 9 quarts

16 cups water
4½ cups sugar
4 cups white vinegar
2 teaspoons salt
1½ packages Mrs. Wages Kosher Dill Pickles mix
2 gallons cucumbers, sliced

1. Mix water, sugar, white vinegar, salt, and Mrs. Wages mix in a large stockpot.

2. Heat on medium until sugar and seasoning mix are dissolved and mixture is just beginning to boil.

3. As the brine is heating, wash and slice the cucumbers.

4. Fill clean, prepared jars with cucumbers, making sure they are full, but not packed in too tightly. (I fill them and tap them on the countertop firmly a few times to settle the cucumbers.) Allow 1 inch of headspace, leaving room for brine.

5. Before pouring the brine over the cucumbers, make sure your canner is full of boiling water, ready to process the pickles.

6. Using a funnel, carefully pour the hot brine into the filled jars, leaving ½ inch of headspace.

7. Wipe the jars and rims, making sure to remove any sticky remnants of brine.

8. Place the lids on clean jars and close them with the jars' accompanying screw bands.

9. Using a jar lifter, place the jars into the canner, making sure they are covered with water.

10. Bring water to a rolling boil and process pickles for 5 minutes.

11. Remove from canner and let set on a sturdy surface for 24 hours. After 24 hours, your jars are ready to be stored. (I remove the screw bands before storing, as I always need them for my next canning project.)

BREAD-AND-BUTTER PICKLES

These pickles are sweeter than the kosher dill type, but the added onions go well with sandwiches.

Yield: approx. 5 quarts

1 gallon thinly sliced cucumbers
2 cups thinly sliced onions
¼ cup salt
4 cups sugar
2 cups white vinegar
1½ cups water
1 teaspoon turmeric
1 teaspoon celery seed

1. Combine cucumbers, onions, and salt.

2. Soak for 3 hours, then drain well.

3. Heat sugar, vinegar, water, turmeric, and celery seed over medium heat until just boiling.

4. Fill clean, prepared jars with cucumber-onion mixture, making sure they are full, but not packed in too tightly. (I fill them and tap them on the countertop firmly a few times to settle the cucumbers.) Allow 1 inch of headspace, leaving room for brine.

5. Before pouring the brine over the cucumbers, make sure your canner is full of boiling water, ready to process the pickles.

6. Using a funnel, carefully pour the hot brine into the filled jars, leaving ½ inch of headspace.

7. Wipe the jars and rims, making sure to remove any sticky remnants of brine.

8. Place the lids on clean jars and close them with the jars' accompanying screw bands.

9. Using a jar lifter, place the jars into the canner, making sure they are covered with water.

10. Bring water to a rolling boil and process pickles for 5 minutes.

11. Remove from canner and let set on a sturdy surface for 24 hours. After 24 hours, your jars are ready to be stored. (I remove the screw bands before storing, as I always need them for my next canning project.)

MUSTARD PICKLES

These pickles are a nice addition to a vegetable or cheese tray.

Yield: approx. 4 quarts

1½ cups white vinegar
3 cups water
1 tablespoon dry mustard
2 cups sugar
1 teaspoon pickling spice
1 teaspoon salt
1 gallon small, whole cucumbers

1. Mix white vinegar, water, dry mustard, sugar, pickling spice, and salt in a large stockpot.

2. Heat on medium until sugar and seasonings are dissolved and mixture is just beginning to boil.

3. As the brine is heating, wash and slice the cucumbers.

4. Fill clean, prepared jars with cucumbers, making sure they are full, but not packed in too tightly. (I fill them and tap them on the countertop firmly a few times to settle the cucumbers.) Allow 1 inch of headspace, leaving room for brine.

5. Before pouring the brine over the cucumbers, make sure your canner is full of boiling water, ready to process the pickles.

6. Using a funnel, carefully pour the hot brine into the filled jars, leaving ½ inch of headspace.

7. Wipe the jars and rims, making sure to remove any sticky remnants of brine.

8. Place the lids on clean jars and close them with the jars' accompanying screw bands.

9. Using a jar lifter, place the jars into the canner, making sure they are covered with water.

10. Bring water to a rolling boil and process pickles for 5 minutes.

11. Remove from canner and let set on a sturdy surface for 24 hours. After 24 hours, your jars are ready to be stored. (I remove the screw bands before storing, as I always need them for my next canning project.)

SWEET DILL PICKLES

Sweet dill pickles, without the kosher dill mix, taste more like a sweet pickle.

———————

Yield: approx. 4 quarts

1 teaspoon dill seed or 1 head fresh dill
1 onion, sliced
1 clove garlic or ½ teaspoon garlic powder
2 cups water
3 cups sugar
2 cups vinegar
2 tablespoons salt
1 gallon cucumbers

1. Heat water, sugar, vinegar, and salt in a large stockpot until sugar is dissolved and mixture is just beginning to boil.

2. As the brine is heating, wash and slice the cucumbers.

3. Fill clean, prepared jars with cucumbers, making sure they are full, but not packed in too tightly. (I fill them and tap them on the countertop firmly a few times to settle the cucumbers.) To each jar allow 1½ inches of headspace for 1 teaspoon or 1 head fresh dill, 1 onion, and 1 garlic clove or ½ teaspoon garlic powder.

4. Before pouring the brine over the cucumbers, make sure your canner is full of boiling water, ready to process the pickles.

5. Using a funnel, carefully pour the hot brine into the filled jars, leaving ½ inch of headspace.

6. Wipe the jars and rims, making sure to remove any sticky remnants of brine.

7. Place the lids on clean jars and close them with the jars' accompanying screw bands.

8. Using a jar lifter, place the jars into the canner, making sure they are covered with water.

9. Bring water to a rolling boil and process pickles for 5 minutes.

10. Remove from canner and let set on a sturdy surface for 24 hours. After 24 hours, your jars are ready to be stored. (I remove the screw bands before storing, as I always need them for my next canning project.)

BANANA PICKLES

Banana pickles are traditional Amish pickles that are often served for lunch following church services. They are cut from large cucumbers and sliced into spears.

Yield: approx. 6 quarts

2 cups vinegar
2 cups water
6 cups sugar
2 teaspoons salt
2 teaspoons celery seed
2 teaspoons turmeric
2 teaspoons mustard seed
1 gallon large pared, deseeded cucumber spears

1. Mix vinegar, water, sugar, salt, celery seed, turmeric, and mustard seed in a large stockpot.

2. Heat on medium until sugar and seasonings are dissolved and mixture is just beginning to boil.

3. As the brine is heating, prepare the cucumbers.

4. Fill clean, prepared jars with cucumbers, making sure they are full, but not packed in too tightly. (I fill them and tap them on the countertop firmly a few times to settle the cucumbers.) Allow 1 inch of headspace, leaving room for brine.

5. Before pouring the brine over the cucumbers, make sure your canner is full of boiling water, ready to process the pickles.

6. Using a funnel, carefully pour the hot brine into the filled jars, leaving ½ inch of headspace.

7. Wipe the jars and rims, making sure to remove any sticky remnants of brine.

8. Place the lids on clean jars and close them with the jars' accompanying screw bands.

9. Using a jar lifter, place the jars into the canner, making sure they are covered with water.

10. Bring water to a rolling boil and process pickles for 5 minutes.

11. Remove from canner and let set on a sturdy surface for 24 hours. After 24 hours, your jars are ready to be stored. (I remove the screw bands before storing, as I always need them for my next canning project.)

REFRIGERATOR PICKLES

These pickles are not actually canned. They are sliced, have brine poured over them, and are refrigerated. They can be stored in the fridge for up to 30 days and are a great way to use a few leftover cucumbers.

Yield: approx. 2 quarts

7–9 cups sliced cucumbers
1 cup sliced green peppers
1 cup thinly sliced onion
2 tablespoons salt
1 tablespoon celery seed
1 cup white vinegar
2 cups sugar

1. Slice cucumbers into a large bowl.
2. Add the peppers and onions.
3. Sprinkle salt and celery seed over vegetables.
4. Mix vinegar and sugar until sugar is dissolved.
5. Pour mixture over vegetables and stir well.
6. Refrigerate and enjoy for up to 30 days.

Pickled Vegetables

CRISP DILLY GREEN BEANS

Dilly beans are similar to pickles but with a different texture. They are a tasty side to barbeques and especially delicious when served ice-cold on a warm summer day.

Yield: approx. 4 pints

2 pounds small, tender green beans
1 teaspoon cayenne pepper
4 cloves garlic
4 large heads dill
2 cups water
¼ cup salt
1 pint white vinegar

1. Destem green beans and pack into jars, allowing 1½ inches of headspace.

2. To each jar add ¼ teaspoon cayenne pepper, 1 clove garlic, and 1 head dill.

3. Heat water, salt, and vinegar until boiling.

4. Pour brine over beans, allowing ½ inch of headspace.

5. Wipe the jars and rims, making sure to remove any sticky remnants of brine.

6. Place the lids on clean jars and close them with the jars' accompanying screw bands.

7. Using a jar lifter, place the jars into the canner, making sure they are covered with water.

8. Bring water to a rolling boil and process green beans for 5 minutes.

9. Remove from canner and let set on a sturdy surface for 24 hours. After 24 hours, your jars are ready to be stored. (I remove the screw bands before storing, as I always need them for my next canning project.)

PICKLED BEETS

Pickled beets is another traditional Amish dish that is served at lunch following church services. These beets are sweet but also sour.

Yield: approx. 10 pints

10 pounds fresh, raw beets
2 cups vinegar
2 cups water or liquid from cooking beets (beet juice)
2 cups sugar
1 teaspoon salt

1. Wash the beets thoroughly.

2. Cut off the leafy tops, but leave the tops of the stems intact. You will remove the tops later. Do not remove the root end, either.

3. Cover the beets with water in a large stockpot and boil until fork tender.

4. Drain cooking liquid, reserving 2 cups for the brine.

5. Cool beets until they aren't too hot to touch.

6. Cut off the tops and root ends and peel beets using your fingers to slide the peels off. Try not to cut into the sides of the beets.

7. Slice or cut beets into chunks and fill jars, leaving 1 inch of headspace.

8. Heat reserved cooking liquid with all remaining ingredients until just boiling.

9. Before pouring the brine over the beets, make sure your canner is full of boiling water, ready to process the beets.

10. Using a funnel, carefully pour the hot brine into the filled jars, leaving ½ inch of headspace.

11. Wipe the jars and rims, making sure to remove any sticky remnants of brine.

12. Place the lids on clean jars and close them with the jars' accompanying screw bands.

13. Using a jar lifter, place the jars into the canner, making sure they are covered with water.

14. Bring water to a rolling boil and process beets for 20 minutes.

15. Remove from canner and let set on a sturdy surface for 24 hours. After 24 hours, your jars are ready to be stored. (I remove the screw bands before storing, as I always need them for my next canning project.)

HARVARD BEETS

You can serve this type of beet as a quick vegetable or side dish to almost any meal.

Yield: approx. 4 pints

1½ cups sugar
2½ tablespoons cornstarch
2½ teaspoons salt
½ cup vinegar
¾ cup water
8 cups cooked beets, sliced or diced

1. Mix sugar, cornstarch, and salt.

2. Add in vinegar and water.

3. Mix well.

4. Stirring often, heat brine over medium heat until boiling.

5. Remove brine from heat and pour over beets.

6. Ladle into jars.

7. Wipe the jars and rims, making sure to remove any sticky remnants of brine.

8. Place the lids on clean jars and close them with the jars' accompanying screw bands.

9. Using a jar lifter, place the jars into the canner, making sure they are covered with water.

10. Bring water to a rolling boil and process beets for 10 minutes.

11. Remove from canner and let set on a sturdy surface for 24 hours. After 24 hours, your jars are ready to be stored. (I remove the screw bands before storing, as I always need them for my next canning project.)

Relishes

Relishes are good condiments to have in stock in your basement or pantry. They taste great with burgers and hot dogs, of course, but also with grilled meats or sandwiches. Relishes take a bit more time than pickles, and the process is a little different, but still perfectly doable. I enjoy making relishes, even if it takes a lot of chopping!

GREEN TOMATO RELISH

This is a great recipe to use up any extra green tomatoes at the end of summer.

Yield: approx. 12 pints

24 large green tomatoes
6 red and/or green bell peppers
12 large onions
3 tablespoons celery seed
3 tablespoons mustard seed
1 tablespoon salt
5 cups white sugar
2 cups cider vinegar

1. Grind or finely chop tomatoes, peppers, and onions.

2. In a mesh sieve or colander, let drain for 1 hour.

3. Combine chopped vegetables with all remaining ingredients in a large stockpot.

4. Boil for 20 minutes.

5. Ladle into jars.

6. Process in hot-water bath for 30 minutes.

ONION RELISH

Yield: approx. 3 pints

14 medium onions
6 medium green peppers
3 small hot peppers, *optional*
4 cups white vinegar
3 cups sugar
2 tablespoons salt

1. Chop or grind onions and peppers.

2. In a large pot, heat vinegar, sugar, and salt.

3. Bring to a boil and add in vegetables.

4. Simmer for 15 minutes.

5. Ladle into hot jars.

6. Process for 10 minutes in a hot-water bath.

PEPPER RELISH

Yield: approx. 3 pints

2 dozen large peppers
15 medium onions
½ cup salt
Boiling water (enough to cover vegetables)
3 cups vinegar
3 cups sugar
1 teaspoon mustard seed
1 teaspoon celery seed
1 teaspoon salt

1. Chop or grind peppers and onions.
2. Sprinkle with salt and cover with boiling water.
3. Soak vegetables in boiling water for 10 minutes.
4. Drain well.
5. Mix vinegar, sugar, mustard seed, celery seed, and salt.
6. Pour over vegetables.
7. Heat until boiling and boil for 15 minutes.
8. Ladle into hot jars and process for 10 minutes.

PICKLE RELISH

Yield: approx. 15 pints

4 quarts cucumbers, chopped or ground
¼ cup salt + 1 teaspoon salt, *divided*
1 quart onions, chopped
1 pint peppers, chopped
2 teaspoons mustard seed
2 teaspoons celery seed
1 teaspoon turmeric
4 cups sugar
2 cups vinegar

1. Chop or grind cucumbers.
2. Sprinkle with ¼ cup salt and let soak for 1 hour.
3. Drain well and add in remaining vegetables.
4. Mix 1 tablespoon salt, mustard seed, celery seed, turmeric, sugar, and vinegar.
5. Pour over vegetable mixture.
6. Bring to a boil over medium heat.
7. Simmer for 20 minutes.
8. Ladle into hot jars and process for 10 minutes.

ZUCCHINI RELISH

This relish takes a bit more time as the vegetables need to soak longer. This recipe calls for soaking overnight, but I have made this relish often, sometimes only soaking for two to three hours, and it turned out fine! This is my family's favorite relish.

Yield approx. 15 pints

12 cups ground or chopped zucchini
4 cups ground or chopped onion
1 large pepper, ground or chopped
5 tablespoons salt
2½ cups vinegar
6 cups sugar
1 tablespoon dry mustard
½ teaspoon pepper
¾ tablespoon cornstarch
¾ teaspoon turmeric
1½ teaspoons celery seed

1. Mix chopped vegetables with salt.
2. Let soak overnight.
3. Drain well.
4. Mix remaining ingredients and pour over vegetables.
5. Bring to a boil over medium heat.
6. Simmer for 30 minutes.
7. Ladle into hot jars and process for 10 minutes.

Jams and Jellies

Jams, jellies, and sweet spreads are a great way to preserve fresh summer fruit. I always make strawberry jam in the spring, as that's our family favorite. I have tried others as well, but strawberry remains the favorite. The one ingredient that you'll definitely have to buy is fruit pectin. Pectin comes in powdered or liquid form and is easy to use. It's just important to remember: Do not try to change the amount of sugar in a recipe, because the jelly will not gel correctly. I've tried that with disastrous results! (We had strawberry sauce that year instead of jam.) There are different versions of most recipes, some are made with liquid pectin, some with powdered pectin, and some are made the old-fashioned way with no added pectin at all. I always use the powdered pectin as that seems to work well. I prefer using Sure-Jell brand fruit pectin, but that's just my preference. I'm sure other kinds work just as well.

A note on freezing versus canning:

Most jam or jelly recipes can be both frozen or canned. The only real difference you'll notice is the color of your product. When you freeze jelly it retains the bright color of fresh fruit. If you can it, the heat of the canner will change the color to a darker shade. They both taste great, so the choice is yours, depending on what color you prefer your jams and jellies.

A note on jam versus jelly:

The only difference in jam or jelly is that jam has pieces of fruit in it and jelly is juice of fruit, so it will be completely smooth with fewer seeds, such as strawberry seeds when making strawberry jelly.

STRAWBERRY JAM

This is my favorite recipe, passed to me from my friend Karen. Since I started using this strawberry jam recipe, it's the only jam we like. We eat it on toast and also paired with sharp cheddar cheese. Even the boys love cheese and strawberry jam! I freeze my jam because I love the bright red color, but you don't have to. It still tastes great canned.

Yield 4—5 pints

2 quarts fresh strawberries
1 box regular Sure-Jell fruit pectin
7 cups sugar

1. Remove stems of strawberries and wash and drain berries well.

2. Crush berries to the right consistency for your taste.

3. Mix crushed berries and Sure-Jell together in a large pot.

4. Stirring constantly, heat on high until mixture comes to a rolling boil.

5. Add in sugar.

6. Cook until mixture returns to a rolling boil.

7. Boil on high for 1 minute.

8. Pour into prepared jars or freezer containers.

9. Let jam set at room temperature for 24 hours before putting in freezer.

10. If canning, wipe rims of jars and add lids.

11. Process in a hot-water bath for 10 minutes.

12. Let cool for 24 hours before storing.

GRAPE JELLY

You can do the first four steps of this recipe the evening before actually making the jelly.

Yield: approx. 9 (8-oz.) jelly jars

5 cups fresh grape juice from 5 pounds fresh
   Concord grapes
1 (1.75-oz.) package fruit pectin
6 cups sugar

1. To make fresh grape juice, wash the grapes well and remove from stems.

2. Heat in a large saucepan with just enough water to prevent scorching.

3. Line a stainless-steel colander with several layers of cheesecloth and set over a bowl.

4. Let drip undisturbed for 2 hours minimum or overnight.

5. In a large saucepan, whisk fruit juice and pectin until pectin is dissolved.

6. Stirring frequently, bring to a boil.

7. Add sugar all at once and bring to a boil.

8. Boil on high for 1 minute.

9. Pour into prepared jars.

10. Wipe rims and add lids and screw bands.

11. Process in hot-water bath for 10 minutes.

12. Let set at room temperature for 24 hours before storing.

RASPBERRY JELLY

You can do the first four steps of this recipe the evening before actually making the jelly.

Yield: approx. 6 (8-oz.) jelly jars

4 pounds raspberries
4 tablespoons lemon juice
1 package powdered fruit pectin
5½ cups white sugar

1. To make fresh raspberry juice, wash the raspberries well.

2. Heat in a large saucepan with just enough water to prevent scorching.

3. Line a stainless-steel colander with several layers of cheesecloth and set over a bowl.

4. Let drip undisturbed for 2 hours minimum or overnight.

5. In a large saucepan, add lemon juice to fruit juice, then whisk in pectin until pectin is dissolved.

6. Stirring frequently, bring to a boil.

7. Add sugar all at once and bring to a boil.

8. Boil on high for 1 minute.

9. Pour into prepared jars.

10. Wipe rims and add lids and screw bands.

11. Process in hot-water bath for 10 minutes.

12. Let set at room temperature for 24 hours before storing.

APPLE JELLY

You can do the first five steps of this recipe the evening before actually making the jelly.

Yield: approx. 6 (8-oz.) jelly jars

5 pounds apples
1 package powdered fruit pectin
5 cups white sugar

1. To make fresh apple juice, wash the apples well and quarter them, removing stem and blossom ends.

2. Heat in a large saucepan with enough water to cover all the fruit.

3. Stirring frequently, boil until apples are softened, approximately 30 minutes.

4. Line a stainless-steel colander with several layers of cheesecloth and set over a bowl.

5. Let drip undisturbed for 2 hours minimum or overnight.

6. In a large saucepan, whisk fruit juice and pectin until pectin is dissolved.

7. Stirring frequently, bring to a boil.

8. Add sugar all at once and bring to a boil.

9. Boil on high for 1 minute.

10. Pour into prepared jars.

11. Wipe rims and add lids and screw bands.

12. Process in hot-water bath for 10 minutes.

13. Let set at room temperature for 24 hours before storing.

PEACH JELLY

You can do the first six steps of this recipe the evening before actually making the jelly.

———————————

Yield: approx. 5 (8-oz.) jelly jars

3 pounds peaches
1½ cup lemon juice
1 package powdered fruit pectin
5 cups white sugar

1. To make fruit juice, wash and quarter the peaches. The pits don't have to be removed, but it makes the boiling process easier if they are.

2. Add 1½ cup lemon juice for each pound of peaches.

3. Stirring frequently, bring to a boil.

4. Boil gently for 20 minutes.

5. Line a stainless-steel colander with several layers of cheesecloth and set over a bowl.

6. Let drip undisturbed for 2 hours minimum or overnight.

7. In a large saucepan, whisk fruit juice and pectin until pectin is dissolved.

8. Stirring frequently, bring to a boil.

9. Add sugar all at once and bring to a boil.

10. Boil on high for 1 minute.

11. Pour into prepared jars.

12. Wipe rings and add lids and screw bands.

13. Process in hot-water bath for 10 minutes.

14. Let sit at room temperature for 24 hours before storing.

ELDERBERRY JELLY

You can do the first four steps of this recipe the evening before actually making the jelly.

———————◦⟨∽⟩◦———————

Yield: approx. 5 (8-oz.) jelly jars

3 pounds elderberries
4 tablespoons lemon juice
1 package powdered fruit pectin
4½ cups white sugar

1. To make fresh elderberry juice, wash the elderberries well and remove from stems.

2. Heat in a large saucepan with just enough water to prevent scorching.

3. Line a stainless-steel colander with several layers of cheesecloth and set over a bowl.

4. Let drip undisturbed for 2 hours minimum or overnight.

5. In a large saucepan, whisk lemon juice and pectin until pectin is dissolved.

6. Stirring frequently, bring to a boil.

7. Add sugar all at once and bring to a boil.

8. Boil on high for 1 minute.

9. Pour into prepared jars.

10. Wipe rims and add lids and screw bands.

11. Process in hot-water bath for 10 minutes.

12. Let set at room temperature for 24 hours before storing.

MINT JELLY

Yield: approx. 5–6 (8-oz.) jelly jars

3 cups water
1½ cups fresh spearmint or peppermint leaves
2 tablespoons white vinegar
⅓ cup powdered pectin
½ teaspoon butter
Green food coloring, *optional*
4 cups sugar
Mint sprigs, for garnish

1. Bring water to a boil.
2. Add mint leaves and turn off heat.
3. Steep for 15 minutes.
4. Strain tea.
5. Add vinegar, pectin, butter, and food coloring (if using).
6. Stirring constantly, mix well and bring to a boil.
7. Add sugar and return to boil.
8. Boil on high for 1 minute.
9. Remove from heat and skim off foam.
10. Pour into jars with a mint sprig to garnish each jar.
11. Wipe rims and add lids and screw bands.
12. Process in hot-water bath for 10 minutes.
13. Let set at room temperature for 24 hours before storing.

HOT PEPPER JAM

Yield: approx. 8 (8-oz.) jelly jars

10 large jalapeño peppers
3 medium red bell peppers
2 medium green bell peppers
1 cup cider vinegar
1 package powdered fruit pectin
5 cups white sugar

1. Chop all peppers and measure them out to 4 cups total.

2. In a saucepan, add vinegar and pectin.

3. Stir well and bring to a boil over medium heat.

4. Add sugar all at once.

5. Return to a boil.

6. Boil on high for 1 minute.

7. Pour into prepared jars.

8. Wipe rims and add lids and screw bands.

9. Process in hot-water bath for 10 minutes.

10. Let set at room temperature for 24 hours before storing.

Old-Fashioned Jams and Jellies

HOT PEPPER JAM (WITHOUT PECTIN)

Yield: approx. 8 (8-oz.) jelly jars

14 cups chopped hot or sweet peppers
¼ cup salt
6 cups sugar
4 cups vinegar

1. Sprinkle chopped peppers with salt.

2. Soak for 3 hours.

3. Do not drain peppers.

4. In a saucepan, add sugar and vinegar.

5. Stirring occasionally, bring to a boil and boil for 45 minutes.

6. Pour into prepared jars.

7. Wipe rims and add lids and screw bands.

8. Process in hot-water bath for 10 minutes.

9. Let set at room temperature for 24 hours before storing.

BLACKBERRY JELLY

Variations of this jelly can be made using different fruits. Just remember to measure the fruit juice after it has drained for at least 2 hours and then add equal amounts of sugar.

Yield: approx. 6 (8-oz.) jelly jars

2 quarts blackberries
3 cups water
White sugar

1. Wash and drain blackberries.

2. Add water and cook blackberries until soft.

3. In a cheesecloth-lined colander, drain berries.

4. Let drip at least 2 hours or overnight.

5. Measure fruit juice and add sugar equal to the amount of juice.

6. Stirring frequently, boil on high until jelly thickens.

7. Pour into prepared jars.

8. Wipe rims and add lids and screw bands.

9. Process in hot-water bath for 10 minutes.

10. Let set at room temperature for 24 hours before storing.

RHUBARB JAM

Yield: approx. 6 (8-oz.) jelly jars

3 pounds rhubarb stalks
½ cup water
4 cups white sugar
2 oranges, zest and juice

1. Cut rhubarb into ½-inch pieces.

2. Place in saucepan with water, sugar, and orange zest and juice.

3. Bring to a boil.

4. Stirring constantly, simmer for 30 minutes.

5. Pour into prepared jars.

6. Wipe rims and add lids and screw bands.

7. Process in hot-water bath for 10 minutes.

8. Let set at room temperature for 24 hours before storing.

Sweet Spreads

PEAR BUTTER

Yield: 8–9 (8-oz.) jelly jars

3 quarts mashed pears
1 quart sugar

1. Peel ripe pears and cook until soft.

2. Drain and mash well.

3. Stir mashed pears and sugar together.

4. Stirring frequently, bring to a boil.

5. Boil on high for 1 minute.

6. Pour into prepared jars.

7. Wipe rims and add lids and screw bands.

8. Process in hot-water bath for 10 minutes.

9. Let set at room temperature for 24 hours before storing.

PEAR HONEY

Yield: approx. 12 (8-oz.) jelly jars

12–14 medium ripe pears, peeled and cored
8 cups sugar
1 (20-oz.) can crushed pineapple
3 tablespoons lemon juice

1. Puree pears in blender or food processor.

2. Stir remaining ingredients into pears.

3. Bring to a boil in a large saucepan.

4. Reduce heat and boil gently, stirring occasionally for 50 to 60 minutes or until thickened.

5. Pour into prepared jars.

6. Wipe rims and add lids and screw bands.

7. Process in hot-water bath for 10 minutes.

8. Let set at room temperature for 24 hours before storing.

EASY APPLE BUTTER

Yield: approx. 5–6 pints

2 quarts applesauce
2 cups brown sugar
1 cup white vinegar
1 tablespoon cinnamon
½ teaspoon cloves

1. Stir all ingredients together, mixing well.

2. Bring to a boil over medium heat.

3. Simmer for 2 hours.

4. Pour into jars and process for 15 minutes.

Soups

Having an array of canned soup in your basement is a great idea. There's nothing easier than grabbing a can of soup for a quick meal.

A note on canning soup:

Most food safety organizations recommend using a pressure canner for soup. My family processes canned soup for 3 hours to make sure it maintains a high temperature all the way through, but if you prefer to use a pressure canner the time is 1 hour at 10 pounds pressure.

CREAM OF CELERY SOUP

This is a condensed-style soup that can be used in recipes as is or diluted with milk or water. You can also substitute mushrooms for the celery and have cream of mushroom soup instead.

Yield: approx. 9–10 pints

3 bunches celery, finely chopped
3 quarts chicken broth
1 cup butter
½ cup onion, chopped
1½ cup flour
1 tablespoon salt

1. Combine celery and broth in a large stockpot.

2. In a separate pan, melt butter and sauté onions until nice and brown.

3. Whisk flour and salt into butter mixture.

4. Stir butter mixture into celery mixture and boil until thickened.

5. Ladle into clean jars, allowing 1½ inch of headspace.

6. Process in hot-water bath for 3 hours.

HAM AND BEAN SOUP

Yield: approx. 12 quarts

1 pound butter
1 large onion, chopped
3 quarts diced cooked ham
2 gallons great northern beans or other beans of
  your choice
3 cups ketchup
2½ cups brown sugar
Salt, pepper, or other seasonings of your choice

1. Melt butter and sauté onion until soft.

2. Add ham and cook for 15 minutes.

3. Pour beans, ketchup, brown sugar, and seasonings into a 12-quart stockpot.

4. Add in ham mixture and enough water to fill stockpot.

5. Stir well and adjust seasonings to taste.

6. Ladle into clean jars.

7. Process in hot-water bath for 3 hours.

CHUNKY BEEF SOUP

Yield: approx. 10–12 quarts

2½ quarts water
2 cups flour
¼ cup beef base or beef bouillon
1 can beef broth
1 quart tomato juice
½ cup brown sugar
1½ tablespoons salt
1 quart diced carrots
1 quart diced potatoes
1 quart peas
1 bunch celery
1 onion, diced
2 tablespoons butter
2 pounds hamburger

1. Whisk water, flour, beef base or bouillon, beef broth, tomato juice, brown sugar, and salt, mixing well.

2. Stirring often, bring to a boil until mixture is thickened.

3. Allow to cool.

4. Sauté onion in butter with hamburger.

5. Combine all ingredients and stir well.

6. Ladle into clean jars, allowing at least 1½ inch of headspace.

7. Process in hot-water bath for 3 hours.

CHICKEN NOODLE SOUP (TO CAN)

Yield: I quart

I cup uncooked egg noodles or 2–3 tablespoons
   uncooked rice
⅓ cup chopped celery
¼ cup chopped or grated carrots
⅓ cup diced cooked chicken
I teaspoon salt
I teaspoon dried onion flakes
Chicken broth

1. Add all ingredients to a quart-sized jar.

2. Fill jar with chicken broth, leaving 1-inch headspace.

3. Process in hot-water bath for 3 hours.

VEGETABLE SOUP

Yield: approx. 16 quarts

1 quart green beans
1 quart sliced or diced carrots
1 quart diced potatoes
1 quart peas
1 quart diced onions
1 quart corn
1 quart lima beans
3 large peppers, chopped
3 pounds hamburger, *optional*
2 tablespoons butter
7 quarts tomato juice
2 tablespoons beef bouillon
¾ cup brown sugar
2 tablespoons chili powder
3 cup alphabet or other small pasta

1. Precook all vegetables and cool before mixing soup.
2. Sauté peppers and hamburger (if using) in butter.
3. Mix vegetables, browned peppers and hamburger (if using) and all remaining ingredients together.
4. Adjust seasonings to taste.
5. Ladle into clean jars.
6. Process in hot-water bath for 3 hours.

Note: Vegetables for this soup can be switched according to personal tastes.

CHILI SOUP

Chili soup is an Amish version of chili that is not as thick or meaty as a typical chili.

Yield: approx. 16 quarts

6 onions
6 pounds hamburger meat
2 tablespoons butter
12 cups kidney beans
9 quarts tomato juice
3 pints pizza sauce or plain tomato sauce
3 teaspoons paprika or more to taste
3 tablespoons chili powder or more to taste
9 tablespoons brown sugar
3 tablespoons Worcestershire sauce
1 tablespoon salt or more to taste

1. Sauté onions and hamburger in butter.
2. Add all remaining ingredients and mix well.
3. Bring to a boil.
4. Ladle into clean jars.
5. Process in hot-water bath for 3 hours.

CONVERSION CHARTS

METRIC AND IMPERIAL CONVERSIONS

(These conversions are rounded for convenience)

Ingredient	Cups/Tablespoons/ Teaspoons	Ounces	Grams/Milliliters
Butter	1 cup/ 16 tablespoons/ 2 sticks	8 ounces	230 grams
Cheese, shredded	1 cup	4 ounces	110 grams
Cream cheese	1 tablespoon	0.5 ounce	14.5 grams
Cornstarch	1 tablespoon	0.3 ounce	8 grams
Flour, all-purpose	1 cup/1 tablespoon	4.5 ounces/0.3 ounce	125 grams/8 grams
Flour, whole wheat	1 cup	4 ounces	120 grams
Fruit, dried	1 cup	4 ounces	120 grams
Fruits or veggies, chopped	1 cup	5 to 7 ounces	145 to 200 grams
Fruits or veggies, pureed	1 cup	8.5 ounces	245 grams
Honey, maple syrup, or corn syrup	1 tablespoon	0.75 ounce	20 grams
Liquids: cream, milk, water, or juice	1 cup	8 fluid ounces	240 milliliters
Oats	1 cup	5.5 ounces	150 grams
Salt	1 teaspoon	0.2 ounce	6 grams
Spices: cinnamon, cloves, ginger, or nutmeg (ground)	1 teaspoon	0.2 ounce	5 milliliters
Sugar, brown, firmly packed	1 cup	7 ounces	200 grams
Sugar, white	1 cup/1 tablespoon	7 ounces/0.5 ounce	200 grams/12.5 grams
Vanilla extract	1 teaspoon	0.2 ounce	4 grams

OVEN TEMPERATURES

Fahrenheit	Celsius	Gas Mark
225°	110°	¼
250°	120°	½
275°	140°	1
300°	150°	2
325°	160°	3
350°	180°	4
375°	190°	5
400°	200°	6
425°	220°	7
450°	230°	8

INDEX

NOTES

NOTES

NOTES

NOTES